Rainier Panorama

by Will Landon

Library of Congress Catalog Card Number 96-94660

ISBN 1-56044-517-3

Printed and bound in Singapore.

Published by Will Landon of Bellevue, Washington, in cooperation with Skyhouse Publishers,
an imprint of Falcon Press® Publishing Co., Inc., Helena, Montana.

Layout designed by Will Landon.
Design enhancements, typesetting, and other prepress work by Falcon Press® Publishing Co., Inc.,
Helena, Montana.

Distributed by Falcon Press® Publishing Co., Inc.
P.O. Box 1718, Helena, Montana 59624
or call 1-800-582-2665

Cover photo: A telephoto panoramic of Mount Rainier from the Eatonville Road.

To my children,

RICHARD, CAROL, BRADLEY, AND VIRGINIA

*They grew up hiking the trails of this majestic mountain
with me and my wife, Pat. They grew in stature at the same time.
The lessons of wilderness became their instructor in determination
and in the discovery of beauty waiting to be found;
they learned to see.*

*T*he willow makes an arch
with new spring growth.
The spirit mountain appears
through a green window.

$\mathcal{T}$he sunrise clouds form a stream of energy radiating from the volcano
dominating this land. The old mountain vented its life-giving outpourings
over the ages, nurturing the earth.

LAKE WASHINGTON

MOUNT RAINIER—1975

PANORAMA OF 100 DEGREES

$\mathcal{T}$he air is clear on this cold winter morning. The mountain is floating on a buoyant skirt of ground-based clouds, while hiding its head in a sky-touched shroud.

$\mathcal{T}$here are many roads to the mountain, all of them small as befits the approach of the humble to the majestic. This grand highway of commerce travels proudly between cities. From it branch the more respectful roads, curving and winding, wrapping around, and even climbing the flanks of the mountain. They take us to where we can explore, becoming servants to our findings.

*T*he monochromes of winter still linger in the high country. Shadows and shades of white and grey prevail. The beginning cracks in the ice of the frozen lake are a sign that the cold nights are surrendering to the warming days of spring.

Soon the first meadow flowers will thrust through the remaining scant coverings of snow to make their official announcement that a new growing season has begun. Their time of renewal is also mine, and I look forward to claiming it.

MOUNT RAINIER

TIPSOO LAKE

$\mathcal{D}$escending from the higher winter-bound elevations, down the narrow winding road with its steep wall of granite, I see the first clumps of early growing grasses. They perch as miniature mesas on steps of fragmented rock.

CHINOOK PASS ROAD

*H*ow little purchase
is required for this hardy
flowering bush on the
vertical granite wall.
I see it here every year
with its vivid display,
and marvel at such an
attainment with so little soil
and so few nutrients. It does
so much with so little.
I am always humbled
in the comparison.

CHINOOK PASS ROAD
ROCK PENSTEMON

7

At sunrise the early sharp light
best defines the flanks and spires
of these rocky projections
against the mother mountain,
which looms behind them.

The mountain is climbed more often,
for it is higher and therefore more
prestigious in the eyes of many. But
for the persons who climb these chimneys
there are satisfactions equal to those derived
from attaining the higher summit.

COWLITZ CHIMNEYS
PANORAMA OF 30 DEGREES

Though it is spring in the lowlands, it is still winter on this high, unplowed road, which we followed on our skis for the length of this day. Now in the late afternoon's light the heavy overcast is breaking apart under the sun's influence, and finally we glimpse the mountain and its flanking buttresses. It is time to make camp, to rest, and to prepare for morning. Perhaps the sunrise will meet our expectations.

MOUNT RAINIER FROM SUNRISE ROAD

PANORAMA OF 100 DEGREES

TAMANOS MTN.

SARVENT GLACIERS

BARRIER   GOVERNORS RIDGE   COWLITZ CHIMNEYS

PANORAMA OF 180 DEGREES

PANHANDLE GAP   MEANY C

*I*n spring the influx of water from melting snow and rain showers quickly reaches a sustained crescendo when compressed through narrow defiles and diverted around and over unyielding boulders. Underlying this accelerated flow is the constant muttering of unseen stones protesting their movement downstream.

In the midst of this torrential force, flitting from rock to rock and bobbing in characteristic style, is a water ouzel feeding on insect castaways.

CHINOOK CREEK

$\mathcal{T}$he water rushing over
the small falls under the bridge
creates a deep sound, that of
a continuously breaking ocean
wave. The containing sidewall
rocks are worn smooth, with
rounded corners and concave
deflecting surfaces. The still
green canopy imparts a gentle
calm in contrast to the
turbulent creek.

CHINOOK CREEK

$\mathcal{D}$ownstream from the cascade
of water was a deep green pool
with a quiet eddy. A place
to compose, then to gather
and pass through another cataract
in the continuing journey that
would end in the ocean.

CHINOOK CREEK

PANORAMA OF 250 DEGREES

$\mathcal{A}$ plunge falls, such as this one, pours a concentrated column of milk-white water into a large saucer-shaped pool, where it quickly becomes green, leaving the white as froth lapping at the side walls. Though hard to see, there are large wise fish idling near the base of the falls, making their selections from the parade of edibles passing by them.

STAFFORD FALLS

FALLS ON OWYHIGH TRAIL CROSSING OF CHINOOK CREEK

PANORAMA OF 170 DEGREES

The antiquity of old trees gives me pause when I pass them on the trail. Well over thirty generations of human beings have lived and died during the lifetime of some of these giants. They began growing at the time of the crusades, and before the settlement of our country. Consider the elements they have withstood in attaining such stature.

Few of the most durable works of man remain intact after a span of only a few centuries, and we marvel at those edifices. These works of the creator abound in this old forest, and they deserve no less admiration.

DOUGLAS FIRS ON EAST SIDE TRAIL

*T*he time for dying of an old tree can be sudden from lightning or a blowdown, or it can be a process taking many years, occurring in gradual increments. The shedding of thick slabs of bark while still standing is akin to the discarding of ceremonial robes in preparation for death.

Mourn not for the going, for there will be a returning. A returning to the earth and a returning of the new out of that soil.

DOUGLAS FIR

$\mathcal{A}$t this one place on the trail could be seen the many stages of a tree's life. There were seedlings, young and mature trees, the dying, the standing dead, and the fallen nurse logs. This was truly an extended family all living in the same house.

PANORAMA OF 150 DEGREES

*M*ushroom colonies are attracted to the sawn ends of trees cleared from the trails that we walk. They are usually a close-knit society sharing a source of common nutrients. They live for a while, arrange for their succession, and then wither and die in place.

The firm density of these specimens testified to their health. Their silver and black coloring made them hard to notice. Theirs was an understated determination.

CONIFER-BASE POLYPORE
(*HETEROBASIDION ANNOSUM*)

*T*he sound of my voice is
not heard in the air that stirs
through this remote ravine.
The insights I perceive and
speak to myself are without
benefit of the constituencies
reserved for the mighty.

My perceptions may appear
wise to me at times, but there is
no forum of any consequence
that would benefit from my
counsel except myself.
Perhaps, if I alone follow these
advisings, that is enough benefit
to merit their speaking.

CHINOOK CREEK FALLS

PANORAMA OF 280 DEGREES

*T*he red heather is wrapped across the top and sides of the tombstone-shaped granite boulder. It is a funerary wreath in commemoration of those who have paid the ultimate price for their love of this mountain.

BURROUGHS MOUNTAIN TRAIL

PHYLLODOCE EMPETRIFORMIS

$\mathcal{H}$ow life clings, finds succor where least anticipated. What is hostile for one is Eden for another. There is a strength in response to adversity, for ease is not handed out here. A paucity of nutrients that is inadequate for most gives exclusive sustenance to these residents.

*T*he mountain remained
hidden behind heavy groupings of clouds
that were slowly responding to the attempts
of the sun to burn through to the waiting
earth below. The blockade of vapor was first
breached at mid-day, and then began
its retraction into the atmosphere.

As the mountain was uncovered to my view
a spot of green announced a lake that is
normally frozen at this time of year.
Both the great and the small
are worthy of notice.

FROM SECOND BURROUGHS MTN.

PANORAMA OF 300 DEGREES

MOUNT RAINIER   THIRD BURROUGHS MOUNTAIN

$\mathcal{A}$ silver streak glistened in the arc of the glacier, marking the icy melt at its highest origins. There is the far away sound of the creek thus formed.

This bowl of ice is an area of desolation to the eye, perhaps, but not to reason. For here are stored vast reserves of water that can be slowly drawn upon for distribution to the valleys below, should the winter's snow pack prove insufficient for the summer's needs.

FROM THIRD BURROUGHS MOUNTAIN

MT. RAINIER & WINTHROP GLACIER

PANORAMA OF 300 DEGREES

MOUNT ADAMS

MOUNT HOOD

MOUNT RAINIER   MOUNT SAINT HELENS

33

$\mathcal{T}$antalizing glimpses of a view are often tendered by the early morning ground fog when the seasons are changing. The cloud may swoop in, rapidly blocking all view, and then just as suddenly rise and fragment into portholes through which the mountain can be seen.

FROM WHITE RIVER VIEWPOINT ON HIGHWAY 410

*W*ith summer come
the leaves: blades filled
with the power of growing.
With summer come the
flowers: petals grouped
with decorations showing.
With summer come the
wanderers: some to
pollinate, some to see.
With summer come the
travelers: the insects,
the animals, you, and me.

INDIAN PAINTBRUSH
(CASTILLEJA PARVIFLORA)

*T*he common goes
unnoticed until a beam
from the sun isolates it
from its dark surroundings.
A sensuous light caresses
each curve and rib with a
voluptuous touch, and when
passing through imparts a
translucent warmth to this
slow dance of the leaves:
a saraband of greenery.

GREEN HELLEBORE
(*VERATRUM VIVIDE*)

There is an innate rhythm to all human endeavor. When discovered, there is a functionality that becomes a song to the task, and as such can be breathed or chanted to make light the work. The climb to the pass, the descent to the flowered meadow below, each has its own chorus to accompany the effort and the visual symphony.

TRAIL TO INDIAN BAR
MT. ADAMS IN DISTANCE

*T*hat which surrounds me can contribute more to my sense of completeness than the salient featured attraction. The encroaching coats of moss, the ravine with devil's club, the rocky beach, the massive stone structures: they are all elements that frame the waterfall.

FALLS ON STEVENS CREEK
PANORAMA OF 270 DEGREES

*T*he water-bonded image is a
deeper-hued copy of the mountain
rising above the tree line of this frigid
lake. There is a magic quietness
in which nothing is heard: no wind,
no call of birds, no sounds of insects.

It is a spell awaiting the kiss of the sun to
break; to shatter the surface with ripples;
to dissipate the fog hovering near the opposite
shore; and to give warmth to the creatures
we will hear in their daily regime.

Another day is beginning.

REFLECTION LAKE

$\mathcal{A}$ picture frame of green branches surrounds this stair-step falls. The water divides, then re-unites, aerated with each rebound from the deflecting rocks. It is a preparing ground, giving onward passage to the confluence of many such contributing streams that form the more purposeful creek.

A stream has the charm of a small child, with uninhibited quirks that cause us to smile.

PICTURE FRAME FALLS
NEAR NICKLE CREEK

*I*n the hottest and driest of summers there is little more than the undergarments of the permanent glaciers to cover the bareness of the mountain. The scoured and bulging rocks attest to the ruggedness of the massive physique.

It is no trifling matter to wrestle with this giant when making passages to the higher elevations. The remaining ice in the glaciers can be impassable. Only the snows of winter can fill the deep crevasses and provide the outerwear worthy of royalty.

MT. RAINIER IN OCTOBER 1994

PANORAMA OF 80 DEGREES

*T*he mood of the mountain seems to change when it gets its new trousseau of snow. It becomes more flirtatious, with good days and see-through cloud gaps, then suddenly capricious and even dangerous with weather changes.

This is no temptress to be trifled with. Approach and retreat with respect, and all will be well. Failure to do so brings disfavor with grave consequences.

FROM NISQUALLY OVERLOOK

44

$\mathcal{T}$he rock steps are carpeted with the same green moss as the flat landing above. The small ferns punctuate each of the two risers with their upper layer of present growth and their lower layers of old spent tendrils forming a skirt.

The steps have an inviting, cushioned look, but I resist climbing them, knowing that this is the work of decades, easily damaged beyond repair.

A silver forest surrounds me. Ghosts of trees that once were, but are no more except as wraiths with pale hue. They are their own tombstones, standing in a cemetery now overgrown with new growth, impatient to reclaim the land with a new generation.

SNOW LAKE TRAIL

MOUNTAIN ASH (*SORBUS SITCHENSIS*)

PANORAMA OF 150 DEGREES

$\mathcal{T}$he field of granite was
so large that it seemed
impossible that it could
have derived from the
cliffs that border the vast
and strangely sterile array.
Seasonal moisture and
freezing had cracked
apart the original cliffs,
now gone, over a period
of time that exceeded the
number of rocks, should
they even be countable.

ABOVE SNOW LAKE

PANORAMA OF 280 DEGREES

$\mathcal{W}$e are all of us flawed, with our cracks and chips fracturing the smooth veneer that we present to view. It is only in the mutual charity between ourselves that we can exist in a way that advances our species. Slip the bounds of that charity, and then we slide back to earlier primitive times.

STEVENS CANYON ROAD

50

𝒯he geometry of the earth and the cliff complement the waterfalls, all bearing a pleasing resemblance to that most graceful of letters, the S.

*I*t is the comings and goings that raise our perceptions the most. Whether to and then from a place of beauty, or to and then from those we care for, it is the departure that sharpens the sweetness with a certain indefinable sadness that preserves the event as memorable.

VAN TRUMP CREEK

PANORAMA OF 360 DEGREES

*I*t is so gratifying to see the determination with which nature rebounds after the earth has been disturbed. It is even more pleasing when the reclamation is fostered by flowering plants.

With these plants there is a double benefit, for the red berries that come later are a favorite of certain birds.

DRAINAGE DITCH—HWY. 123
BUNCHBERRY
(CORNUS CANADENSIS)

$\mathcal{T}$he foxglove and the daisy have a luminous glow on a cloudy, bright day in the Northwest. Considering the frequency of such weather in this region it is fortunate indeed that we can enjoy such an attribute.

CARBON RIVER ROAD

55

Summits of mountains must feel it is their duty to waylay the passing airborne moisture, form a cloud, and then retain it in shy retreat.

On this day I marveled at a very unique colonnade of lenticular clouds that had formed in multiple layers from the winds sweeping over the summit. It remained thus for hours, appearing neither to grow nor to dissipate. In reality it was doing both at the same time in a manner imperceptible to the eye.

MOWITCH LAKE ROAD

*T*he dried watercourse belies its true role as a collector of the rain that drained from the meadow earlier in the year. The moisture that had been absorbed stimulated the growth of this flowery display. There was the hum and bustle of insects following their trade routes, negotiating an exchange at every port of call.

SPRAY PARK

LUPINE AND INDIAN PAINTBRUSH

It is the quality of the prior years that accounts for the bloom of the beargrass. Its dry tough leaves discourage all but the goat, vole, pika, and marmot. This phalanx of blossoms appears in military array, but will soon be decapitated with relish by the local residents.

$\mathscr{R}$arely found in the woods
this lone blossom of beargrass
caught a shaft of late sun
penetrating the steeply sloped
forest. Because it was much
taller than many of its cousins
in the meadows, I wondered
if it was older than its kin.
Here, deep in the woods,
there would be few of the
animals that would feed on
its ivory-colored head.

ON THE EUNICE LAKE TRAIL

XEROPHYLLUM TENAX

60

$\mathcal{W}$hy do we labor to climb to the heights only to look down at the place where we have come from?
Simply put, we wish to expand our horizons, look beyond the close at hand,
and see to infinity. That is reason enough to climb to the heights.

VIEW FROM TOLMIE LOOKOUT OF EUNICE LAKE AND MOUNT RAINIER

PANORAMA OF 200 DEGREES

*T*he dial of a glacier's clock has the same twelve subdivisions as our timepieces. Instead of minutes and hours for the big and little hands, the glacier's clock has months and years.

Each fall I climb to this promontory, and it appears that nothing has changed. In fact, the scene below me is in continuous change, but at a pace that will span my generation before it becomes significant to the eye.

WILLIS WALL

CARBON GLACIER

PANORAMA OF 260 DEGREES

RANGER FALLS
PANORAMA OF
135 DEGREES

$\mathcal{C}$oming to this same place year after year, I always receive the same feeling of satisfaction. Though conditions may change, there is an underlying quiet beauty that refreshes and sustains me for another march of seasons.

*W*ould that I could reflect

on what is happening now from

the view point of a decade from now.

It is hard to see ahead clearly.

How many decisions would I change;

how many wrong turns would I not take.

Fortunate is the person who can stand back

and put events into the perspective of history.

Because such insight is so rare, it is best to

choose the path of honor and fairness,

and then tread that path.

SPRAY CREEK

SPRAY CREEK

PANORAMA OF 155 DEGREES

$\mathcal{Y}$our dreams die before you do,

so pursue, pursue, before your

stores of time and energy dwindle

to a fruitless level. Husband the spending

of that fragile hoard in your custody

to attain some measure of accomplishment.

There are not enough lifetimes to apply

to the "could be's" of the truly driven.

SPRAY FALLS

*I*t is late summer, and a drier time. The thunder of the water and its outspray of mist has diminished, inviting a closer approach to this wondrous falls.

Tracings of the former broader flow are on the mossy rocks that lie beyond the current limits. The top of the falls is hidden behind the tumbling curtain that appears to come as a gift from the sky.

SPRAY FALLS

PANORAMA OF 290 DEGREES

*I*t comes as a surprise to many to discover that there is a rain forest in one corner of the park. There are trees draped with moss and swampy areas requiring a board walk. The mix of plant life adapted to these wet conditions provides considerable contrast to the higher alpine growths.

CARBON RIVER RAIN FOREST

$\mathcal{T}$he filtered sunlight permeating the canopy of trees provided a soft light that gave some definition to the many elements of this scene. It must have been thus in the ancient swamps when vegetation was luxuriant, died, and then was pressed into the forest floor to form a deep bog.

CARBON RIVER RAIN FOREST

*I*n this one section of the rain forest there were at least six types of moss growing within yards of each other. Some were on stumps, others on the ground, each having a location suitable for its needs.

I was attracted to this layered brocade where the small mushroom was struggling to make its presence known. It was isolated from others of its kind, but seemed to be doing well on its own.

CARBON RIVER RAIN FOREST

There are occasions in our lives when we speak in ex cathedra clarity. Profound words that reflect a gift of wisdom from a source higher than ourselves. Perhaps at such special times we are a channel being used to guide someone in need of such words. It is a humbling experience.

THE YELLOWSTONE CLIFFS   *PANORAMA OF 145 DEGREES*

Beyond the Yellowstone cliffs and beyond Windy Gap, there is a trail to the only natural bridge in the park. It is on such steep ground that I wonder how anyone could have found it.

Only the early afternoon light ever falls on the arch of the bridge, and that for only a short time. Its location is truly "tucked around the corner."

NATURAL BRIDGE

LAKE JAMES

$\mathcal{T}$here are illusions
that occur during
magical moments of light
in high thin air.
For this is a fey place where
such visions can come
to one's mind.

TOKALOO ROCK

$\mathcal{T}$hose who climb the mountain know this route well, for it is the overnight stopping place before making the climb the next morning.

CAMP MUIR   *PANORAMA OF 360 DEGREES*

A clouded stream wends its way down the former glacier-filled valley. Each zig and each zag tells only part of the story; that of a normal runoff using only a fraction of the capacity of the entire main channel.

The wide distribution of boulders tells us of a time when this was all covered with ice. Under the right conditions a torrent of water can still fill the channel, an awesome sight.

NISQUALLY RIVER

$\mathcal{N}$ature has a way of reminding us that it is pre-eminent. Though we build roads, it can wash them out. Though we build towns, it can flood or shake them down. These overt actions are all reminders of the homage we must accord to the movements of water, wind, and earth.

AFTERMATH OF A JOKULHLAUP DEBRIS FLOW FROM SOUTH TAHOMA GLACIER   *PANORAMA OF 180 DEGREES*

*T*he water grass cannot stand or function without the amniotic lake.
As summer fades it must bend with the ever-shallowing depth,
until all is gone and it can stand no more. Drying, it breaks on the last remembered bend.

*W*hen I walk the shore of my island by the sea of time that stretches beyond my sight,
I claim the respite that is found in the calm waters of solitude.

On this day a grey fog was so dense that there was no perceivable promise of a break.

Near sunset a draft of air sucked the mist down the valley for a few brief minutes, revealing the mountain.

Then with the speed of an ocean wave it returned and all was grey again.

EMERALD RIDGE

PANORAMA OF 360 DEGREES

*T*he death of the tree is
being transformed into the
life of the mushroom
apartment complexes that
inhabit its trunk. They
wax strong for a while and
then wane, giving out an
ooze as they themselves
complete their life cycle.

A year from now only
their whitened skeletons
will remain as they share
the same grave as their host.

LAKE GEORGE TRAIL
SULFUR SHELF
(LAETIPOROS SULPHUREUS)

*M*ost of what we are,
what we know, becomes lost
to those who follow us, even
to our children. Whether it is the
technical knowledge or the living
patterns of earlier generations,
the accelerating impact of change
discards much of value,
never to be reclaimed.

The shape of this dead tree
suggests some great weight
held it in check for a considerable
period of time. What that trauma
was is no longer apparent,
though the determination of the
tree to shed the restraining force
and to rise upwards is evident.

AT LAKE GEORGE

*I*t is near sunset and the winds have begun to shift. The fog trapped in the valley all day stirs, then begins to travel upward toward the branching valleys that come down from the mountain. It begins to twist and turn in the manner of a predator in pursuit, moving faster and faster.

FROM GOBBLERS KNOB

*I*n a few minutes the fog has traveled up to where I am and will soon envelop me. "Now," I say to myself, and freeze the moment on film. Then all becomes grey, for I am consumed.

$\mathcal{T}$he best glow is off the mountain, and the light is becoming more and more diffuse. Harsh contours are softening and a tinge of color touches the clouds. The roar of the river undulates, now strong, now diminished, according to the play of the breezes.

Evening has announced its coming.

NORTH PUYALLUP RIVER

PANORAMA OF 115 DEGREES

$\mathcal{A}$n Ent is rumoured to be a cognitive tree,

capable of communication and activity.

That this is fiction may well be,

but you would have a hard time

convincing me.

With his space alien visage, and penetrating stare,

he made known his message, bidding me most fair.

How this was communicated I don't know,

I only know that it is so.

SILVER FOREST AREA

$\mathcal{A}$ whisper of a trail wends through the silver forest toward the mountain that I seek. Though the trace vanishes entirely from time to time, I press on through the ghostly trees in the direction of the ridge ahead. It only matters that the direction is right, though the way is not always clear.

THE SILVER FOREST

PANORAMA OF 280 DEGREES

$\mathcal{T}$he challenge of the remote place rewards those who achieve it with a treasure house of memories, and an awareness that all is well. Visiting the seldom-traveled corners of wilderness requires a self-reliance that exhilarates, thus enhancing the benefit all the more.

I am happiest when I am exploring. Whether in the wilderness of nature or in the endeavors of my craft, the creative solution, the exploration, that is the thing that excites me the most.

Discovering this pond entirely encircled with golden grass was a moment to remember. The slanting afternoon light angled through each blade, defining it with translucent clarity.

IN A CORNER OF WILDERNESS

*T*he twice determined tree
exhibits the kind of spunk
we can all admire.
First, it had to endure
an adverse germination
in a rocky crevice. Next,
it had to grow downward
to escape its rocky prison.
From there it had to change
direction in order to rise
towards the sky.

Its double adversity was
gracefully overcome.

ST. ANDREWS TRAIL

*W*e usually find mushrooms
growing in conditions of decay
in shaded damp ground,
or on dead and fallen trees.

I was most impressed with the
accommodations chosen by
this citizen. In the background
was a living red cedar tree
with an unusually fine bark.
The forest floor was a
cushiony green growth
that was color coordinated
to the mushroom itself.

There was an elegant
quality to this habitat.

ST. ANDREWS TRAIL
KING BOLETUS
(BOLETUS EDULIS)

$\mathcal{T}$he mountain stands
unmoving and solid,
bathed in the sunset light.
A faithful image is
replicated on the lake
until a whiff of wind
tickles the water,
creating ripples.

Playful distortions occur
on the quivering surface in
random locations, now here,
now there. We are seeing
a rendering from a
fractured kaleidoscope.

AURORA LAKE

*A*ll day long there had been a grey overcast extending beyond vision, and low enough to hide the top of the mountain.

Suddenly the ball of the sun sank below the cloud ceiling revealing a crack on the horizon. The red alpenglow began quickly, illuminating the glaciers before dispersing in the suspended moisture.

The rainbow was a radiant carillon of silent bells extolling the majesty of this wilderness cathedral, and praising the architect and builder.

INDIAN HENRY'S HUNTING GROUND

*V*ine maples congregated on an open hillside only attract our attention in the fall, after going unnoticed during the growing season. It is ironic that the leaves must die before we notice the living tree that remains.

NEAR ROUND PASS

PANORAMA OF 260 DEGREES

Oregon grape leaves can develop a split personality in the fall. One half may decide to make the color change before the other half. When the color changes it may be to yellow or red, or some combination of both.

It is an amusing exercise when the cold weather begins in the fall to look for the most outlandish color combinations of this schizophrenic plant.

TRAIL TO GOLDEN LAKES
MAHONIA

*W*e are so often trapped by our circumstances. To change our course is a very difficult thing to do, for we must confront ourselves. There is a comfort in continuing to do what we now do, an ease in repeating proven cycles.

We can learn from this curious mushroom. It remains hidden in its own underground silo until nearly fully grown. When ready, it thrusts upward, dislodging the forest floor, making its dramatic entrance to the outside world. It cannot go back into the protection of the earth. Its decision is irrevocable. So should ours be, when we change course.

ON OWYHIGH LAKES TRAIL
RUSSULA BREVIPES

SILVER FALLS

PANORAMA OF 360 DEGREES

The shapes of mushrooms can stir the imagination when trying to describe them in field notes prior to their proper identification by a more knowledgeable person.

Rarely would the expedient descriptive name that I jotted down in my field notebook turn out to be the popular name. It did in this case, for I called it a "coral" mushroom, which is its popular name.

CORAL HYDNUM
(HERECIUM ABIETIS)

What else could this be called but "The old woman who lived in a shoe"? A narrow band of light was moving clockwise through the woods as I raced to set up in the shaded light, adjusting the movements of the view camera as best I could. When the light burned across the log end and on the "shoe," I had barely enough time to make several exposures. It was the highlight of that day's outing.

RED BELTED POLYPORE
(FOMETOPSIS PINICOLA)

*T*his cluster of mushrooms
reminded me of a high-rise
apartment house.
I have seen illustrations
of stacked dwellings
in children's books that
looked quite similar.

HONEY MUSHROOM
(ARMILLARIA MELLEA)

$\mathcal{T}$hese were called the
"Trumpets," owing to their
shape. Stray strands of
weak sunlight kept playing
through this intimate scene
from horn to horn.
At just the right moment
a flicker of light settled
on the top "trumpet,"
catching its solo.

GOMPHUS KAUFFMANII

107

$\mathcal{F}$all is the graduation season for spring and summer. As with any graduation there is a celebration, a colorful pomp and circumstances.

PINNACLE PEAK TRAIL   *PANORAMA OF 145 DEGREES*

*T*his natural fortress has steep sides that would make it easy to defend.
The formidable rock structure with its nearly vertical walls has the band of colorful fall
vegetation as its moat. The fog swirls around the defenders manning the ramparts.

STEVENS CANYON

$\mathcal{A}$long the river are
flat pools that form a quiet
surface to reflect the changing
seasons. The shaded water
does this best, for it can add
a contrast that water open
to the sky cannot do.

OHANAPECOSH RIVER

The branch appears to be moving against the current, parting the water with its prow. To the river it is only an obstruction to be cleared from the channel. To me, however, the ripples of wavering designs in the golden reflection are a delight to observe.

OHANAPECOSH RIVER

*T*his tree's life spans a millennium. We have finally learned the value of these ancient beings; they are now venerated, and we benefit. Perhaps in time we will give the same honor to our old ones.

GROVE OF THE PATRIARCHS

WESTERN RED CEDAR

*T*here is a mutuality of support
that is symbolized by this tightly grouped
cluster of trees. Together they are stronger
than their separate states.

GROVE OF THE PATRIARCHS
WESTERN RED CEDARS

113

$\mathcal{T}$rees must answer to the forces of each season, responding with ancient patterns that insure their survival. That one appears to be failing is evident in this grouping. Circadian rhythms of living rooted in prehistory govern us as well. That some are culled should be no surprise.

GROVE OF THE PATRIARCHS   VINE MAPLES, DOUGLAS FIRS, WESTERN RED CEDARS   *PANORAMA OF 160 DEGREES*

$\mathcal{T}$he radiant young upstarts on the edge of the clearing cast a cheerful glow upon their somber elders.
Children of all beings bring a playful brightness into the serious business of living.

GROVE OF THE PATRIARCHS   VINE MAPLES, WESTERN RED CEDARS   *PANORAMA OF 160 DEGREES*

GROVE OF THE PATRIARCHS

PANORAMA OF 360 DEGREES

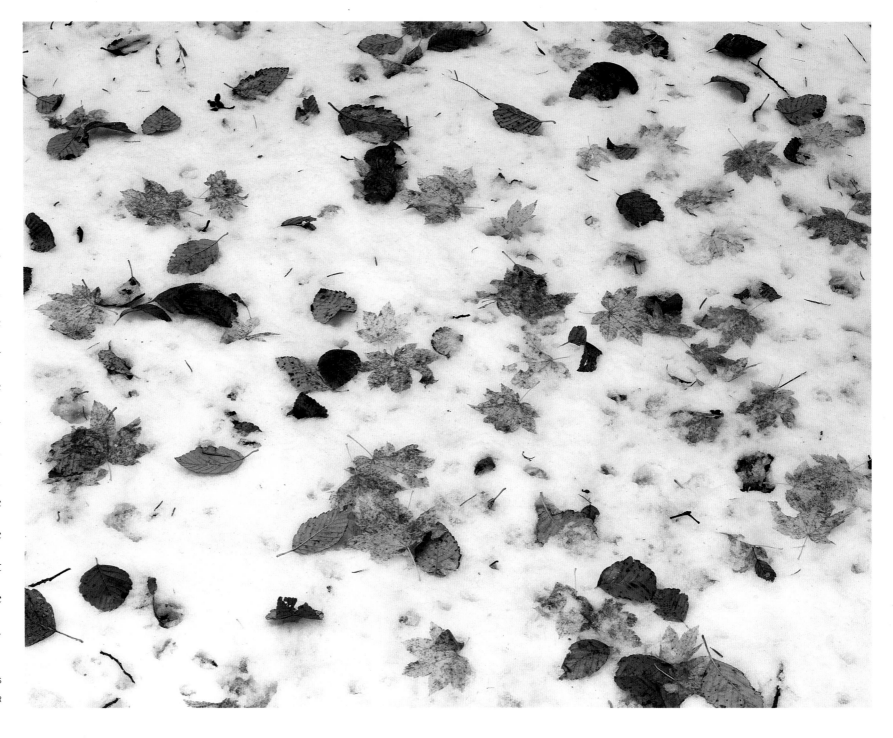

$\mathcal{N}$ature buries her own, each according to its chosen plan. These leaves falling on the first snow have fluttered down in random patterns, to be gripped by the slush. They will be covered until the spring thaw, and then form the mulch that turns to soil.

Their mixed array is more pleasing to the eye than the geometric uniformity that we practice when we place our loved ones to rest.

GROVE OF THE PATRIARCHS
VINE MAPLE AND ALDER

(TOP)

*I*deas clamor for attention, thrust to the forefront with vociferous arguments by their advocates.

Only until they are proven right or wrong in the crucible of history will their noise subside.

Thus it is with the coming of the peak of any season, whether spring's muted symphony,

summer's effulgent growth, fall's garish outpourings, or winter's monochromes;

each must speak forth to be heard.

CHRISTINE FALLS

PANORAMA OF 140 DEGREES

I am eager to listen, for I am willing. For those who are unwilling, the full crescendo is needed to get their attention, and once obtained, the season can retreat, its message having been heard.

CHINOOK CREEK DRAINAGE

VINE MAPLES, PACIFIC SILVER FIRS

PARADISE RIVER

PANORAMA OF 90 DEGREES

*H*ow ancient is this land. The molten rock welling out during the foundation times congealed into the base upon which the earth's future was built. When exposed to view as it is here, it bears the frozen water from the ground above, which forms a tear.

This is a weeping suspended momentarily in memory of all that has passed on the soiled surface sustained by the rock. The collective happiness and sorrow of countless generations of living beings: they are the progenitors for such a copious reminder.

SOUTH PUYALLUP DRAINAGE

ANDESITE LAVA COLUMNS

*W*inter's domain has its own

unique observances when

responding to the rule of cold.

Rain changes form to snow

and floats down slowly

on parachutes of white;

water becomes hard enough

to walk on, though with

difficulty of step; ice

sublimates to vapor without

first becoming a liquid;

waterfalls wear an outer coat

colder than themselves as they

continue to flow in secret.

NARADA FALLS

SIX ICE CLIMBERS

$\mathcal{T}$he first onslaught
of winter fails to dampen
the glow of fall's celebrating
colors. On the contrary,
the white ground covering
eliminates distracting detail,
and adds contrast to the
bright array.

CHINOOK CREEK DRAINAGE
VINE MAPLE

$\mathcal{T}$he later, more burdensome snows make their icy greetings. They subdue the earlier vibrancy into a pale and muted goodbye. Winter's conquest becomes complete. The hope of spring's resurrection is not evident, existing only as a prophesy.

CHINOOK CREEK DRAINAGE
VINE MAPLE

The hoarfrost has transformed the forest floor into a painting, with its many fine brush dots touching every elevated surface. It is a fine, structured pointillism that reveals the veins by leaving them untouched.

This fragile artistry survives only a short time with its enthralling delicacy, and then it is gone, leaving only a haunting memory of winter's lace.

CREEPING RASPBERRY
(RUBUS LASIOCOCCUS)

*H*ow much like a millipede
is the fern appearing to crawl
across the hillside.
The anthropod is noticed
when it moves its double
paired legs in lock step.
The fern is noticed when
its divided leaflets put
on their new coats of frost.
The many on the one
capture our interest.

SWORD FERN
(POLYSTICHUM MUNITUM)

𝓜an is alone; birth and death are solo entrance and exit bows in a one-act monologue.
Man is alone; a captive within a body, he can change or cure, ever so slightly.
Man is alone; a receiver and a giver of countless ideas, he can impress ever so lightly.

NEAR PARADISE ON THE NIGHT OF A FULL LUNAR ECLIPSE - 1983   *PANORAMA OF 360 DEGREES*

$\mathcal{T}$he first snow circumscribes the lake as a white border within a frame of trees.

The prolonged cold forms a tenuous crust that reaches further with every freeze.

The skim ice encroaches upon the reflection, dulling it into a long hibernation.

REFLECTION LAKES

PANORAMA OF 140 DEGREES

$\mathcal{T}$he low, ground-covering mists become more frequent in the increasing cold.

They float the mountain, now trapped in a basket of clouds. Stern reminders to depart are on every hill,

giving fair warning that delay has its price, if unheeded.

FROM BACKBONE RIDGE

$\mathcal{T}$he tracks of a careful rabbit show that it has crossed the exposed area in a crooked manner to deter any predator from the sky or near at hand. Its cities of refuge will get less and less as the snow deepens and smooths to a roundness over the brush; yet it will manage.

$\mathcal{S}$now is truly a coat of many colors.

For white can be white, or it can be yellow, blue, orange, pink, or red,

depending on the mood of the providers commanding the changes.

𝒯here is so much to discover in this wilderness for those who are patient and seek to find it.

𝒾*t can be a lattice of green, decorated with red berries and mushroom terraces.*

BUNCHBERRY
OR DWARF DOGWOOD
(CORNUS CANADENSIS)

DYE POLYPORE
(PHAEDUS SCHWEINITZII)

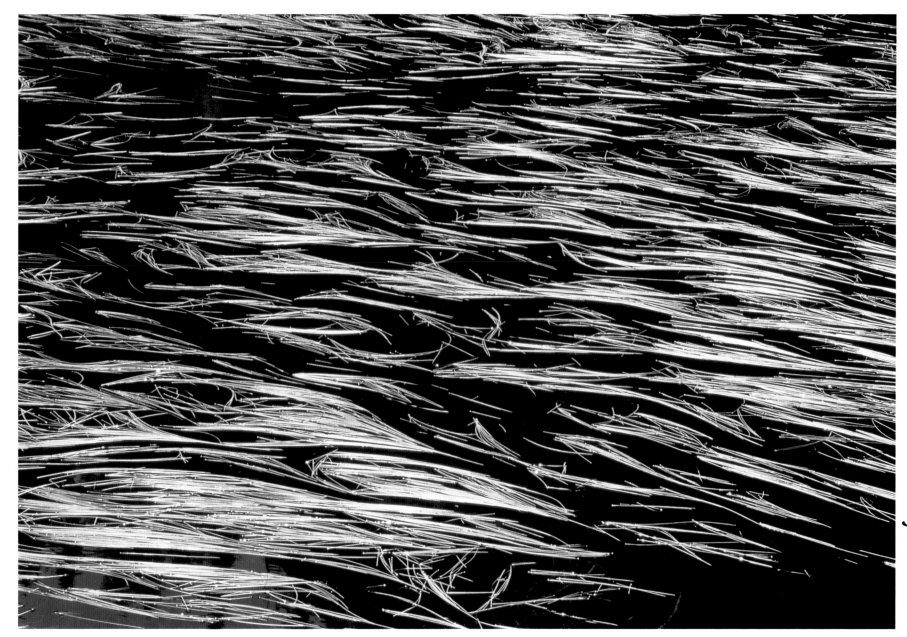

$\mathcal{I}$t can be the patterned
starkness of water grass
highlighted by the
strong morning sun.

$\mathcal{I}$t can be a high vista above a sea of clouds

lapping at the shores of the higher ridges and peaks.

MOUNT ADAMS   MOUNT ST. HELENS

PUYALLUP GLACIER AND EMERALD RIDGE

PANORAMA OF 360 DEGREES

*I*t can be the
crossover from fall
to winter, co-existing
at different elevations.

*I*t can be an edge
of the mountain's
cloud cap lingering
in place for hours.

FROM ST. ANDREWS TRAIL

$\mathcal{I}$t can be the broad leaves of the devil's club and its red berry flower moistened with morning dew.

MARTHA FALLS TRAIL
OPLOPANAX HORRIDUM

*I*t is these never-ending
discoveries that bring me
back again and again
to search them out.

WILD STRAWBERRY
(FRAGARIA VESCA)

$\mathcal{P}$erhaps for the same reason, I, as a visible, mortal, imperfect man, seek again and again

an invisible, immortal, and perfect creator; and though infinitely different, I find in my moment in time

a meaning in being part of a whole that is beyond my comprehension.

The story behind the photographs

WILL LANDON ON SNOWY PEAK

When our family was being raised, "Let's go to the mountain" meant going to Mount Rainier and doing a hike. This could mean a day hike or an extended backcountry trail hike. When I was a scoutmaster, our winter outings were at Cayuse Pass and our fifty milers were on the Wonderland Trail.

Photography was always a part of every trip to the lakes and hills, which we visited as often as we could. Fortunately I used Kodachrome which survived without detectable change from the 1972 weeklong scout hike that resulted in four of the images in this book, on pages 37, 75, 96, and 140.

There was much "sherpa" help in carrying the heavy equipment once I moved into large format and panoramics. Besides my family, there were friends who helped out many times. They were Larry English, Byron and Loren Ponten, Ken Williams, Norm Ibrahim, Phil Araujo, Jerry Hoffman, and Rob Lex. Rob is the lone figure on page 128.

I wish to thank Ranger Ed Wilson for his cooperation which helped me get the winter panoramics on pages 10-13. Thanks to Rangers Mike Dedman and Gene Casey for their advice and cooperation that led to the panoramic on pages 90-91. Panoramic photography often requires the machining of special parts and adapters. A special thanks to my friends Marvin Perrin, Jim Lipari, Thom Thompson, Bill Ponten, and Paul Snyder for doing all those peculiar machining jobs that expanded my capability to capture and produce many of the images in this book.

My main still camera was a 4x5. The grand scenes were often taken on an 8x10 camera. These were supplemented by a Mamiya 645 and a 35mm camera with macro lenses. The majority of the panoramics were taken on rotational equipment capable of 360 degrees. Some subjects required a 6x17 back on the 4x5 camera. A swing lens panoramic camera was needed twice. The second image in the book was taken on my very first panoramic camera, which took five photos on a roll of 120 film. I made it from two spliced-together Kodak 1A Brownies.

I used transparency films for most of the standard format photographs and some of the panoramics. Color negative film was used on all the rotational panoramics due to the extremes of light. This entailed a great deal of darkroom work in order to bring out the best of each subject.

I appreciated very much the expertise of Joy Spurr for the identification of mushrooms, and Joseph and Margaret Miller for the identification of other plant life.

I wish to make a special acknowledgment of the vast storehouse of support supplied by my wife, Pat, who loves to hike as much as I do. She knows what it takes to get a good photograph and then what it takes to put the collection together into a book. The word "helpmate" has a special meaning to us, for this truly was a team effort. ❧